Turning Candlesticks
With Mike Cripps

Text written with and photography by Jeffrey B. Snyder

Schiffer Publishing Ltd

4880 Lower Valley Road, Atglen, PA 19310 USA

Book Design by Laurie A. Smucker

ISBN: 0-7643-0469-0
Printed inUnited States

Published by Schiffer Publishing Ltd.
4880 Lower Valley Road
Atglen, PA 19310
Phone: (610) 593-1777; Fax: (610) 593-2002
E-mail: schifferbk@aol.com
Please write for a free catalog.
This book may be purchased from the publisher.
Please include $3.95 for shipping.
Try your bookstore first.

We are interested in hearing from authors
with book ideas on related subjects.

Dedication

To my good friend Mac Kemp, who is an inspiration to all woodturners.

Contents

Foreword

I have known Mike Cripps for many years and it is a particular pleasure to introduce him to you as the author of this book. He is a big hearted, jovial and highly talented turner who is particularly suited to lead you through the techniques he describes.

Mike and I first met at one of his early woodturning meetings held at a local Cricket Club. His enthusiasm for turning and willingness to help others encouraged a lot of members to improve technique and try other projects.

About a year later, after a lot of hard work, Mike became one of the founder members of the A.W.G.B. (The Association of Woodturners of Great Britain) which was launched in 1987 at the first Loughborough seminar.

In 1990, after being made redundant, Mike decided to set up his own turning school/wood and tool store. This has been a great success and hundreds of aspiring turners have passed through his classes, some now winning competitions, a tribute to Mike's teaching skills and encouragement.

The project in this book is good practice for any turner - just follow Mike's superb instructions and enjoy your turning.

Mac Kemp
Chairman
Middlesex Woodturners Association

About This Book

The traditional candlestick

The first project in this book involves making a candlestick (or a pair of them) based on a traditional design. You will need two pieces of wood, one for the stem and one for the base. A full-size drawing of the candlestick is included. If you copy and paste this to a thin board, as shown, it will provide you with a useful template for transferring the dimensions and setting the design out on the wood mounted on the lathe. This is essential for repetitive turning of a single design.

Repetitive turning is not so difficult as it first seems. If you make a few candlesticks, setting the design out as you go (as illustrated in the book), you will soon be pleased with the results. Remember, the best way to become proficient in turning anything is to make ten of them!

I am sure no one will mind if there are slight variations in the size of the beads and the coves in your first pair of candlesticks. However, if this does concern you, put them at opposite ends of a longer shelf until you have improved a little!

Use some good quality seasoned hardwood. It is a good idea to consider the furniture in the room in which you intend to use your candlesticks. I purchase the brass inserts or cups which hold the candles from America as I am unable to find a supplier in England.

The Triple Candlestick

I love making these clusters of candlesticks from one length of natural timber in the round. In the gallery pictures at the back of this book you will see some triple candlesticks made from Yew wood which is one of my favourite timbers.

The bark can be left on the base of the outside edge where it makes a lovely contrast both in colour and texture with the smooth and polished turned parts. It is quite alright to use part-seasoned timber but a further drying out period will be required following the dividing and roughing-down processes.

A number of options are possible to make your designs even more interesting and attractive to look at. They may all be the same height or varied. The stems may be ornately turned or plain. You can turn the candle cups from the wood or use metal inserts or factory made candle holders. The finished candlesticks look good arranged in a cluster or facing alternative ways in a line.

Basic Turning Tools

The ROUGHING GOUGE, as the name implies, is used for roughing down square to round. It is also used for the preliminary shaping work on spindle turning e.g. shallow curves and tapers. I find that it is an excellent tool for flat areas when face plate turning as well.

A 3/4" roughing gouge is the ideal tool to start with. The approach to the wood should be as follows. Place the roughing gouge firmly on the tool rest with the blade pointing upwards. Lower the tip of the tool down slowly until the bevel rubs on the wood without the cutting edge coming into contact with the wood (this is what I call the no-cut position). Continue to lower the cutting edge down onto the wood until you obtain the first sign of a shaving. Only when this is obtained should you travel along the tool rest from left to right and vice versa to true up the wood between centres.

The PARTING TOOL is an essential tool. I would suggest that a 1/8" wide parting tool is the best to start with and will be the cheapest for spindle turning. The parting tool is used to make incisions into the wood at each end of a piece to provide a waste end which is discarded when the piece is parted off the lathe.

This tool can be used in two ways but when making deep parting cuts or grooves, always ensure that you make the cuts slightly wider than the tool so that it does not get gripped. One method is pointing the tool upwards while sitting it firmly on the tool rest and pushing it in an upward direction. A second method is to start with the tool again sitting on the rest and slowly levering the tip downwards using the tool rest as a fulcrum. NEVER go below the level position and point the tool downwards as it could be pulled in towards the wood and jammed against the tool rest.

The parting tool is also useful for rolling beads and cutting recesses for chucks on faceplate work. If the parting tool is used on its side, flat on the tool rest, the point can be used for scoring decorative grooves in the wood using this scraping cut.

SPINDLE GOUGES come in a range of sizes from 1/8" to 3/4". Most commonly today they are made from round section bar but traditional or continental gouges are still being produced. These are made from pre-formed curved section steel.

The main uses for the spindle gouges are for forming beads and coves, rounding over and squaring up end grain. I would suggest a 3/8" is a good one to start with.

When cutting coves or hollows, point the centre of the gouge at the starting point, cutting down one side to just past the centre of the bottom of the cove and then repeat the process on the other side. By cutting down the hill, or from the largest toward the smallest diameter, you will be compressing together the fibres in the wood with the bevel while the cutting edge does its job. This will give you a good finish. Cutting uphill separates the fibres and leaves an inferior finish. REMEMBER, if you slowly swing the end of the handle in a circular motion, the shape of the cove will also have a round profile. To cut beads or balls, the tool has to be rolled over working again from the top toward the bottom with the bevel rubbing.

The SKEW CHISEL is probably the tool that takes a fair bit of practice before it is mastered. I would suggest that you purchase a 1" OVAL SKEW as this is a size that is good for planing and making beads and squaring ends. An oval skew is nicer to handle than a rectangular section skew as the corners tend to stick on any nicks or grooves in the tool rest.

To plane a cylinder to a smooth finish, raise the tool rest to centre height and position it as close as possible to the pre-roughed out cylinder. Place your thumb firmly on the tool rest just past the end of the wood and tuck the skew between the thumb and the tool rest. Now, using the short corner of the skew and not using any more than 1/8" from the point, the tool should be about 45 degrees to the wood. Obtain a shaving and travel along the tool rest. You may have to alter the angle of the tool or raise or lower the blade slightly. REMEMBER the shaving is the reward and the sign that you are cutting correctly. You will be able to cut coming back along the tool rest by holding the tool at the same angle.

To form beads with the skew I prefer to use the long point and as when cutting only use the actual point and up to 1/8" from it. NEVER cut uphill. Start at the top of the bead, rolling the skew over as it cuts through 90 degrees with the blade vertical on completion of the cut at the base of the bead. When making beads or spheres, work on the right then the left, repeating the process and bringing on both sides together. REMEMBER when cutting over beads etc., rub the bevel all the way — lifting the handle up as the cutting action goes down.

The BOWL GOUGE, as the name implies, is the tool for turning bowls. A 3/8" hisgh speed gouge made from 1/2" round steel with a long and strong handle is the best size to buy. I maintain a bevel of approximately 45 degrees and remove the sharp corners the makers provide by grinding two long blades on the top of the gouge.

Although I love to use the bowl gouge for spindle turning, particularly for long flowing curves for goblets and vases, its main use is for bowls and facework. It is important to constantly rub the bevel to support and steady the cutting edge around external and internal curves. Cutting with the tip unsupported by the bevel makes it 'grabby' and prone to digging in.

To find the right position, lay the bevel on the wood (making sure the tool is firmly on the tool rest) so that you are in the 'no cut' position. With the bevel in contact with the rotating wood, slowly raise the handle until a shaving appears. Stay with it and guide it along or round the surface of the object you are making. You will soon appreciate the supported feeling that the bevel provides as the gouge tip cuts. REMEMBER, if you are changing the shape of the wood from a square corner to a curve, it is much easier if you cut away the corner to a wide chamfer first. To cut wood without the bevel rubbing is like driving a car without wheels!

All the tools that I have just written about are cutting tools which are usually used in an upward mode with the SKEW chisel being the exception as by raising the tool rest it is usually used mainly with the toolrest in the 'level with centre' position.

I would strongly recommend that you buy good quality tools. For the tools we have discussed so far — ROUGHING GOUGE, PARTING TOOL, SKEW CHISEL, SPINDLE GOUGE and BOWL GOUGE — I feel that it is worth the extra cost to purchase high speed steel. Tools of high speed steel will hold their edge up to five times longer and will not be affected like carbon steel by overheating from the electric grindstone.

The last of the basic tools to talk about are SCRAPERS, which are mainly used to remove any bumps and ridges left after using the Bowl Gouge. A scraper is used in a downward position with the tool rest set back from the work to give room to use it at this angle. When sharpened correctly a sharp burr of metal stands up proud on the end of the tool which will produce plenty of shavings.

I have found that carbon steel scrapers, which are less expensive than high speed steel, work extremely well. The burr can be raised by pressing a hard metal bar across the end of the scraper which forces the cutting edge burr upwards (this is known as using a ticketer).

Scrapers can be made in different shapes. For faceplate work a square ended scraper, say 1" to 1 1/4" across with the corners relieved to allow the movement of the tool from the centre to the edge of flat surfaces and vice versa, is ideal. By grinding the corners back slightly, snagging is avoided when in use. For inside bowls and open vessels a 1" to 1 1/4" ROUND NOSED SCRAPER is ideal. The metal should be as sturdy as possible to avoid vibration when cantilevering inside a bowl on the tool rest.

Sharpening the Tools

The SKEW CHISEL and the PARTING TOOL only need re-grinding occasionally and honing with a slipstone is all that is required but keep them sharp at all times. A slipstone made from metal impregnated with diamond dust is an effective way of sharpening them.

I sharpen the end of the ROUGHING GOUGE to a shallow bevel of approximately 45 degree - REMEMBER, although useful for turning softwood etc. long bevels are more grabby for beginners to use. Be very careful to keep the blade straight across by rolling the tool over on the grinding wheel from one corner to the other. A common fault with new turners is only to sharpen the rounded part of the cutting edge which, if done for several sharpenings, forms two long points like cats ears on the gouge.

I sharpen the SPINDLE GOUGE to a finger nail shape with a bevel angle of somewhere between 45 degrees to 60 degrees. If you hold the gouge upwards and rotate it on the grindstone from left to right you will very quickly form a sharp point on the Spindle Gouge and lose the rounded profile. To avoid this rotate the tool, sharpening from centre to right following the existing finger nail shape. You will find that in doing this when you start (with the handle straight and in line with the grindwheel) when you finish the handle will be approximately 45 degrees to the right of you. Now repeat this process from the centre to the left. ALWAYS use only light pressure — only a small touch on the stone is required. It is a good idea to practice this manoeuvre with the grinder switched off first.

The BOWL GOUGE is sharpened in much the same way but if you want the cut back profile I use on my bowl gouges, start from the middle and, following the edge of the tip profile, roll the gouge right over so the flute is facing the wheel, pushing it upwards. Then, to sharpen the cutback section, sharpen as before going toward the other side.

I always use SCRAPERS with the manufacturer's name uppermost so I know which way to use it; however, when sharpening these tools on the grindstone, I turn them upside down. Because the stone is rotating toward you and downwards, it naturally forms a good burr on the bottom edge of the tool which, of course, becomes the top when you use it.

Your grindstone should be kept at a sensible height so that you can use it without stooping. Mine is about 4' from the ground. It is a great help to have an anglepoise light on the stone. The following safety tips should be observed:

(1) NEVER use a grinder without eye protection e.g. visor, goggles or safety glasses. I find that those little clear plastic windows that are provided very soon get scratched and become impossible to see through.

(2) NEVER work on a grindstone that is clogged or out of true. Diamond Wheel Trimmers are much less expensive now and they clean the stone and trim it in just a couple of passes. REMEMBER a clean stone cuts cooler and sharpens efficiently. Take precautions by wearing a mask when trimming the stone as a large amount of dangerous dust is created when this is done.

(3) NEVER ever use your grindstone on soft or non ferrous metals such as copper or brass. If the stone is clogged with this type of material it can overheat with use and even shatter.

An alternative method for sharpening tools now being sold by a major British tool maker consists of wooden discs mounted on an arbor with aluminium oxide abrasives adhered to them. These can be held in a chuck on the lathe and you can clearly see what you are doing. The recommended speed is around 1400 r.p.m on a 5" disc.

Using the Lathe

Spindle Turning (or Turning Between Centres)

As a general rule I prefer to turn small diameter work (say up to 2" x 2") at a fairly fast speed. If you are reducing square stock to round, this makes the task quicker and avoids excess vibration being transferred through the tool to the joints in your hand.

Let us assume you have a piece of square timber mounted securely between centres. Select a speed of around 1200 to 1500 r.p.m. If we look at the pulleys contained within the headstock when selecting our turning speed, it is important to note that the smaller the size of the pulley, the faster the speed of the lathe will be. Put on your visor or safety goggles — ALWAYS PROTECT YOUR EYES.

Always avoid inhaling wood dust when sanding. Use a mask and an extraction unit. An airstream helmet is good but will not prevent a build up of fine dust in your workshop.

To mount the wood between centres when I am teaching, I use a ring centre or friction drive as opposed to a 2 or 4-prong drive. This method is safer because if you have a 'dig in' the wood will stop rotating and slip on the centres. A pronged drive keeps on going regardless and a heavy 'dig in' will result in chunks of wood flying off or the whole piece leaving the lathe. If you do not possess a friction drive, reduce the tension on the drive belt. This will also provide a safety mechanism.

Adjust your tool rest to around 1/2" below centre. Rotate the wood by hand before switching on to make sure it clears the tool rest. Then check all securing levers or nuts including the headstock swivel (applicable on rotating head lathes only) — the tool rest support to the lathe bed — the tailstock to the lathe bed and finally the securing lever to the quill of the tailstock.

Using a 3/4" or 1" Roughing Gouge, point the cutting edge upwards away from the rotating wood onto the tool rest. NOTE — NEVER place any turning tool onto the wood unless the tool is firmly on the tool rest first. Now, gently lower the tip of the gouge until the bevel (flat area next to the cutting edge) is rubbing on the rotating wood without cutting. As lightly as possible (I call this the no-cut position), and still with the gouge on the rest, lift the back hand up and look for the finest of shavings. Use only light pressure toward the wood and obtain a light buzz from the cutting edge as you ease the tool along the tool rest and back.

Stand in nice and close to the lathe with your feet apart and use body movement to move the tool from left to right and vice versa. REMEMBER, outstretched arms are wobbly things. Keep the inside part of your arm against your side and move the tool along with body movement only. As soon as a gap of, say, no more than 1/2" appears between the tool rest and the wood, stop the lathe and move the tool rest in as close as you can while checking that the wood rotates freely without rubbing on the tool rest.

Switch on and, while looking at the horizon (top edge of the wood), make a nice smooth cylinder. Do not allow the tool to swing — this will give you a bad shape. Obtain a shaving, keep the tool at this angle, and move along the tool rest.

General Information On The Lathe And Woodturning Tools

A ring centre, seen in place here on the lathe, is the best centre for beginners. It is most forgiving if you have a dig in.

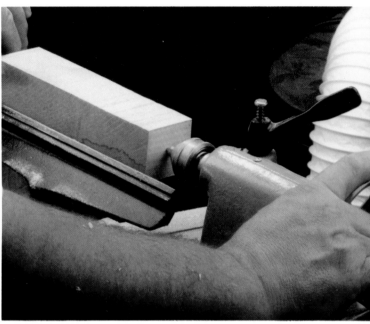

Use an awl to mark the centre of the blank with a small hole. On softer woods, tighten up the tail stock to that centre mark until the drive centre grips. For a harder piece of wood, we might have to tap the centre with a hammer to begin to drive it into the wood.

The smaller the pulley on the headstock, the faster the work is going to go.

Before you turn on the lathe, rotate the wood by hand to make sure that it is not hitting the tool rest. The top of the tool rest should be positioned approximately 3/4" below the centre. This height will vary according to the diameter of the timber, the height of the lathe, and the comfortable working postion the turner wishes to adopt.

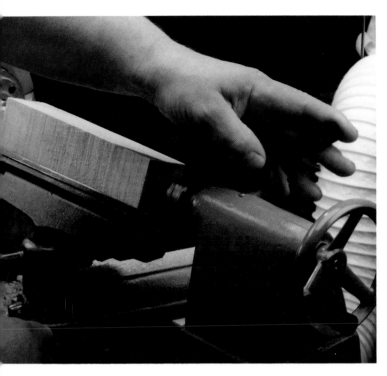

Double check all of the locking handles to the tail stock and the tool rest, making sure they are tight. This precaution will help you avoid accidents. If your lathe is of the swivel head type, make sure the swivel nut is tightened as well. Otherwise, the head could turn while the wood is spinning.

The Roughing Gouge:

The tool should be kept straight across at its cutting edge. I will explain this in detail later when we cover tool sharpening.

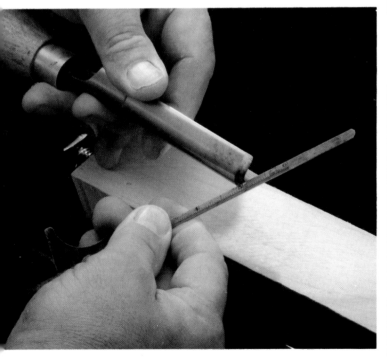

Let's look at the tools now. The first of the tools is the roughing gouge. For people first learning to turn, the roughing gouge is much easier to use if the bevel edge is kept short, approximately at 45 degrees. Longer bevels may be preferred as a turner become more experienced. But in the hands of someone new to wood turning, a long bevel is both grabby and more difficult to use.

Begin with the tool in the "no cut" position.

9

Raise your arm, lifting the handle until the blade just touches the wood and begins to form shavings.

If you travel too fast, rifling will occur. Spiral grooves are created all along the wood.

Slowly move along the length of the wood. Only light pressure is required with a sharp tool. As you move along the wood, roughing the corners off, all you should hear is a light buzz. That is the sign that you are doing the job correctly, making a nice spray of shavings as you go. Keep the tool firmly on the tool rest. Ensure that the bevel of the tool is always rubbing against the wood as this stablizes the tool for you and makes it safer to handle. Also, with the bevel rubbing, your tools will not need to be sharpened as often. Someone new to woodturning tends to stand a long way out from the lathe and work with arms extended. This position tends to make the tool vibrate and wobble, making it hard to get a nice finish. Move in close. Keep your lower arm (the one holding the lower part of the handle) resting against your body, using your body to move the tool back and forth.

Remember, the slower you go, the nicer the finish, half of the rifling has been removed in this picture.

The Parting Tool:

A good parting tool to start turning with is a 1/8" parting tool. Later on, you may feel like investing in a diamond profile 3/16" parting tool (seen on the left) which moves more easily through the wood, without a tendency to be gripped. The diamond profile is, of course, also a much stronger tool for deeper cuts.

The roughing gouge is mainly used to reduce square stock to round and to true up unbalanced timber. However, the roughing gouge is also a useful tool for shaping curves and hollows. Always work down the hill (from the largest to the smallest diameter). By doing this, you are compressing the fibers of the wood together and cutting the wood as it likes to be cut; cutting uphill will separate the wood fibers and give you an inferior finish.

While parting the wood, never allow the tool to fall below the centreline position because it can be pulled in by the rotating wood and get caught between the wood and the tool rest.

The approach to the wood, as before, is from a high position with the bevel rubbing. Lift the handle upwards and lower the cutting edge gently down onto the surface of the wood. Continue cutting into it, then go back to the starting position again and take a second cut along-side the first to widen the groove. This will prevent your tool being grabbed in a narrow parting cut. The first use of this tool is to remove the scrap wood from either end of the piece. There are two reasons for doing this. One is to remove the marks left by the drive and live centres and the other is to ensure that the wood is cut away on the end of the piece of timber. This area is often full of small hairline cracks where it has dried.

The second method of using the parting tool is with it sitting firmly on the tool rest, the bevel rubbing, pushing upwards only. Again widen the groove as before to keep the tool from getting gripped.

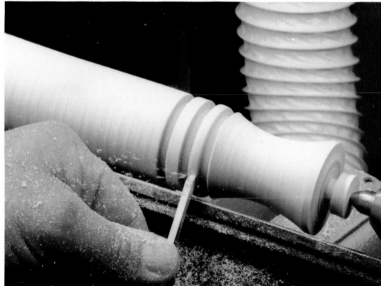

Cut down the diameter of the waste wood so that it is a little larger than the lathe centres. This will keep the waste wood out of our way, giving us better access to the ends of the wood.

The parting tool is also very useful for forming beads. The wider the parting tool, the easier it is to use for this function. Make two shallow grooves, one on either side of the proposed bead. Place the parting tool with the bevel rubbing in the centre of the bead-to-be and, with a rolling action, roll over to the right two or three times until you have rounded over the square corner on the right.

The Spindle Gouge:

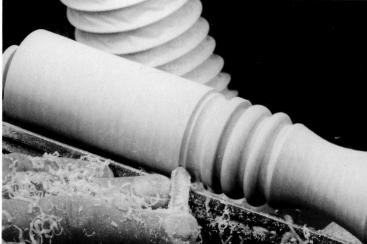

Then move to the left to round the other side. Remember, always look at the horizon to obtain the best view of the shapes you are making.

The parting tool has one other useful function. Placed on its side, flat on the tool rest in a downward scraping mode, it is excellent for making fine decorative lines and grooves.

The spindle gouge is used for generally shaping wood, forming coves and beads, and can be used to clean up end grain. The best spindle gouge for beginners is the 3/8". To make a cove, start with the bevel rubbing, supporting the cutting edge, and swing the handle in a perfect circular motion. If the handle travels in a circle, your cove will be round. Smooth flowing actions are the secret of nice shapes.

With the parting tool, we can further enhance the appearance of the cove by cutting two small shoulders, one on either side. This gives the cove a classical look often found in beautiful and period furniture.

The Skew Chisel:

Raise the tool rest to the lathe centre height or just above centre to use the skew chisel.

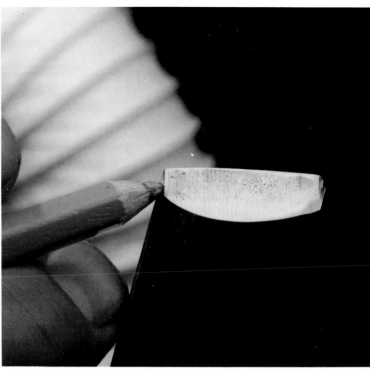

I would suggest you buy a 1" oval skew chisel. You will find this tool much nicer to handle and much smoother to run along the tool rest than the old style square edged skew chisel. The square corners tend to catch in all the marks in the tool rest. The oval chisel glides across them.

Use the short corner of the skew for planing the wood. We are only going to use the area 1/8" from the short corner. Do not cut with the higher part of the blade.

15

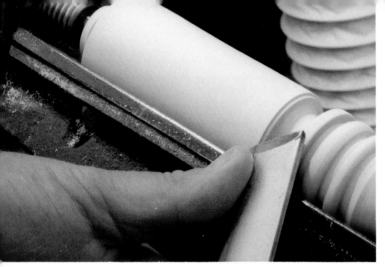

First put your thumb slightly to the right of the starting position on the tool rest. Lay the bevel of the tool on, raising a shaving just above the short corner.

Slide the tool along the tool rest in a planing action. If the tool jutters and doesn't run smoothly, either raise or lower your back hand slightly or change the angle of your cut very slightly. When you feel it is right, continue with the planing action.

The skew chisel is used for rounding over ends, forming balls and beads. To round the end you must rub the bevel along the edge of the wood.

Using the skew chisel to make beads.

I am using the skew chisel to make a ball. Work first to the right and then to the left, bringing the ball into shape on both sides equally.

The Round Nosed Scraper:

Buy a 1" or 1 1/4" round nosed scraper manufactured from good, sturdy metal. The scraper doesn't have to be made of high speed steel. The round nosed scraper, used in the downward angle, is ideal for cleaning up, removing tool marks, smoothing down troublesome end grain, and is invaluable when face plate or bowl turning.

The Bowl Gouge:

A 3/8" bowl gouge is a good size to start with in your tool kit. You can see how large it is.

Sharpening the tools using an electric grinding wheel:

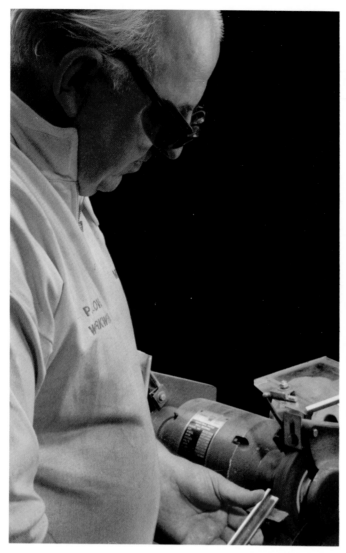

Sharpening the roughing gouge. Make sure the top is straight across.

It is essential that your grindstone is fixed at a sensible height where you can view what you are doing without stooping. Standard work bench height is far too low for most people. The grindstone should also be well lit. The light is an essential aid when examining a tool for sharpness; a blunt section of the blade will reflect light and a sharp section will not. I prefer not to use the manufacturer's see-through shields. I find they soon become scuffed and marked and are very difficult to see through. Always wear safety goggles or glasses while working on the grindstone. This is very important. Always ensure that your grinding wheel is running true and that it is clean. Both of these conditions may be achieved with the use of a diamond (or other form of) trimmer.

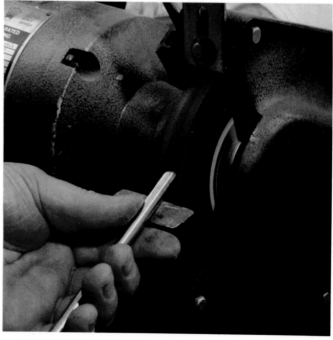

Sharpening the spindle gouge. Refer to the notes in the general material for further sharpening details.

Turning Candlesticks

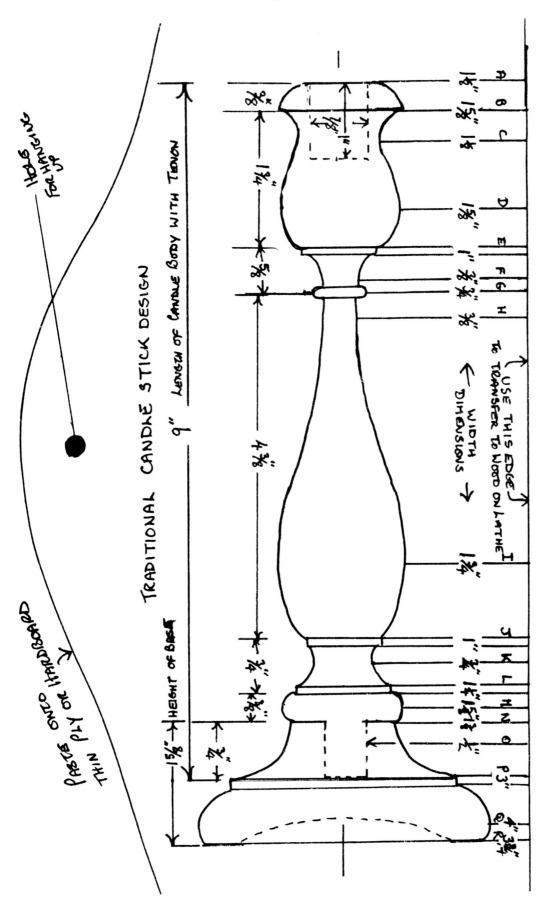

Traditional Candle Stick Design

Hole for hanging up

Paste onto hardboard thin ply or hardboard

9" Length of Candle Body with Tenon

Height of Base

Use this edge to transfer to wood on lathe

Width dimensions →

We will begin by turning a traditional English candlestick in American Black Walnut. We are using two pieces of wood. The block for the stem measures 2" x 2" x 9 1/2" long. The disk for the base measures 4 1/2" x 2" thick.

Using a /8" bowl gouge, reduce the wood to a 4" finished diameter. Make su the bevel is against the wood and the flute in the gouge is at appro nately 45 degrees. Stop just short of the end to the wood so as not to c .ip the end grain.

Drill a hole about 1" deep into the base disk. This hole will be drilled to size to fit whichever screw chuck you have. These vary from one manufacturer to the next.

Coming back from the other direction, pick up the ridge you left at the end of the previous pass and move back across the wood.

Fit a woodscrew bit into the chuck body of the lathe. Screw the base onto the bit. You may lock down the chuck to use two hands for screwing on larger pieces.

Check to make sure that the disk measures 4" in diameter. Notice that I have beveled the edges of the disk to avoid hurting my hands on rough edges.

Use the 3/4" roughing gouge to clean the face of the disk

The wood face is clean.

Here is a common problem. A dimple is formed if you cut below the centreline of the disk.

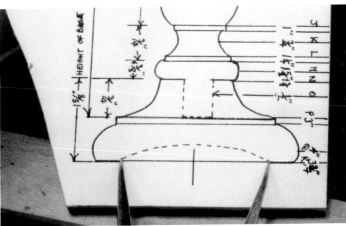

Measure the length of the hollow in the base of the candlestick foot from the template.

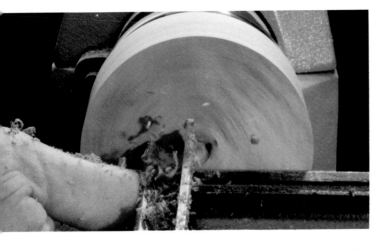

Come back up to the centre and you will be able to quickly clean off this dimple.

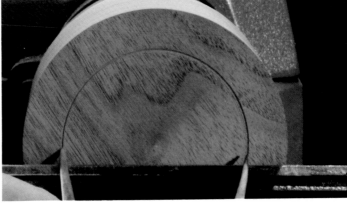

Transfer the measurement to the base of the candlestick, keeping the left leg firmly on the tool rest. The right leg does not touch the wood. If that tip of the divider should touch the wood, the rotation would drive the tip over, following the upward rotation of the disk.

The domed recess under the foot.

Mark out the perimeter of the recess with a parting tool. Make a channel twice as wide as the parting gouge. Hollow out the underside of the foot using a 3/8" bowl gouge. A 3/8" spindle gouge would work just as well. To create the hollow, move in sweeping motions left to right with the bowl gouge.

Use the parting tool and bowl gouge as before, now make another recess to fit the expansion jaws of the chuck. This recess will vary in size according to the type of wood turning chuck you have. If this recess is cut neatly and not too deeply, it is easily removed afterwards. Begin the process by marking off the diameter with the dividers.

Cut in 3/32" with the parting tool.

Make a small mark in the centre of the recess with an awl. This centre mark will be useful when the candlestick is assembled to accurately remount it between centres. At that later stage we can also remove the chuck recess together with the centre mark. There is no point in sanding the bottom now because we know we have further work to do in this area later.

Undercut the side of the recess with a skew chisel or a diamond shaped scraper. Undercutting the side allows you to match the tapered shape of the wood chuck jaws, which will prevent the work from pulling off of the lathe.

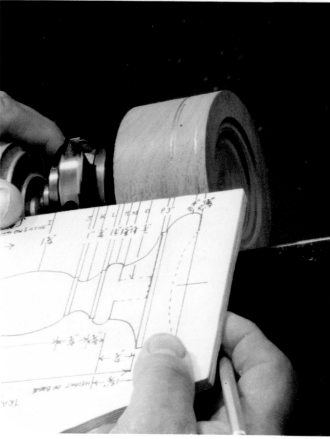

Place the pencil against the wood, turn on the lathe, and the mark is extended around the wood disk.

Using a pencil and your template, mark in the placement of the details on the disk.

24

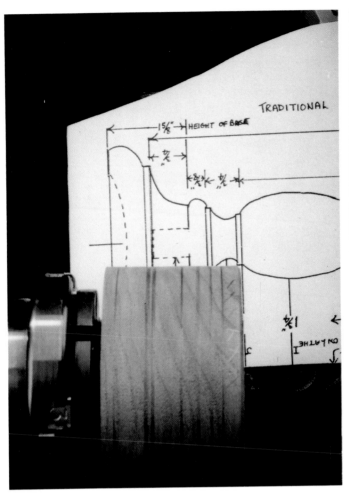

Remove the base from the screw chuck, turn the base around, and fit it into the chuck jaws in the recess created before. If you can prop up your template behind the work, it will give you a very handy reference. The X's on the wood mark the waste wood on the disk.

Using a parting tool, cut the wood to fit the calipers and form that shoulder. Make sure to widen the gap so the parting tool will not bind. Remember to round the tips of your calipers to avoid them catching in the wood. Also, if you do not feel comfortable measuring the space with the calipers while the lathe is running, you may turn off the lathe each time you wish to check.

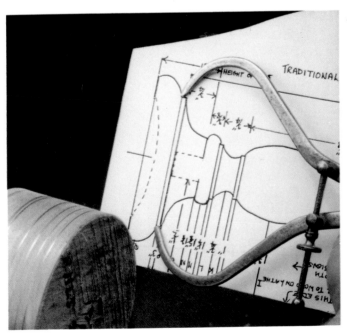

Set the calipers to the first shoulder, which is dimension P on the template and measures 3" in diameter.

Using the parting tool, round down both sides of the base's bottom edge.

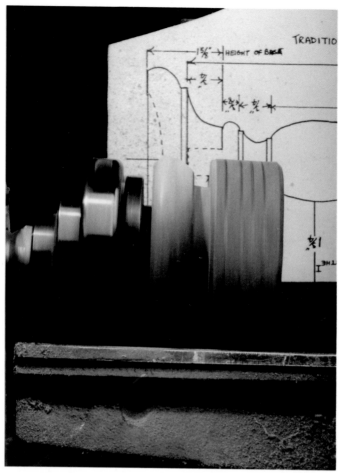

Reduce the top end of the base to the correct height (mark N on the template) using the roughing gouge.

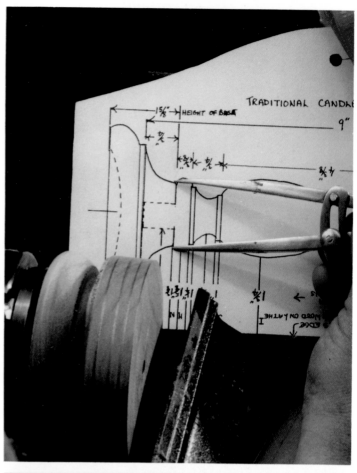

Smooth down the end of the wood disk.

The width dimension of point N is marked onto the end of the wood using a pair of dividers.

Mark a sweeping curve from the shoulder at P to the top of the base at item N. Please note that item O applies to the size of the tenon on the top part of the candlestick itself. Reduce the wood using the bowl gouge placing the tool rest at an angle. First cut off the corner. This makes it much easier. Then cut down to an angle before adding the curve. It is easier to curve an angle than it is to curve a square edge.

Remark the shoulder at position P.

Complete the external curve with the spindle gouge.

Like this.

Remove any rough marks with the burr on the inside of the spindle gouge.

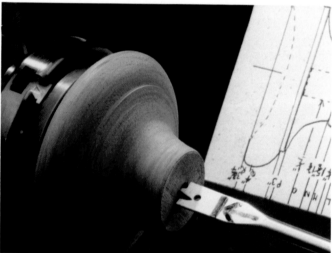

Drill in a hole for the tenon about 3/4" deep with a 1/2" drill bit.

Make a long sweeping curve with the spindle gouge, rubbing the bevel as you go.

Sand the base, using progressively finer grades of cloth backed abrasive strips. Make sure to fill the strips with wood shavings to keep the heat from burning your fingertips. Use a dust extractor while sanding to keep your lungs and shop clean.

Apply wax to the base to give it a glossy surface and polish it.

Apply Danish Oil or a sealer to the base.

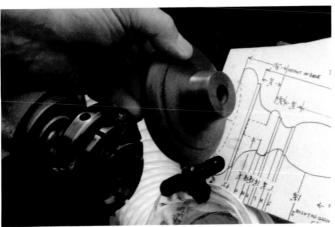

Remove the base from the chuck.

Dry the oil with a paper towel.

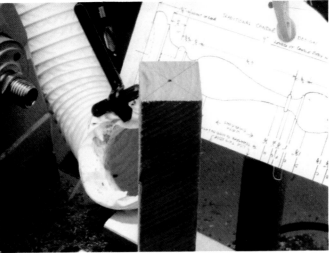

Add the live centre to your tail stock and a drive centre into the head of the lathe to prepare to turn the stem. Mark the centres of the end of your wood stock and put in a small guide hole with an awl.

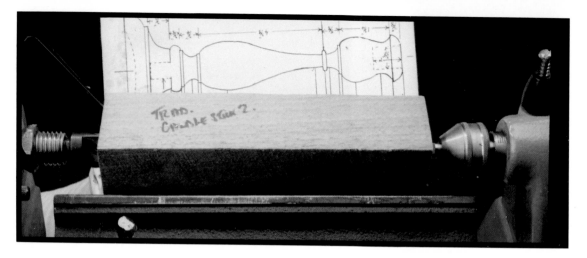

Attach the stem to the lathe and place your tool rest just below centre, taking care to make sure the wood does not rub against the rest before you begin turning. Always rotate the wood by hand before switching on the lathe.

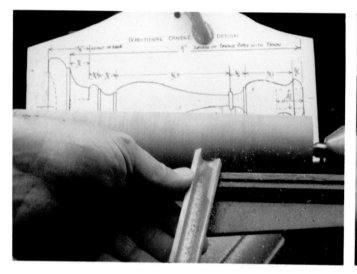

Begin roughing down the wood with a 3/4" roughing gouge. Remember to work lightly here and, as the wood rounds, to keep the bevel against the wood. Round down about 3/4 of the way to the finished shape.

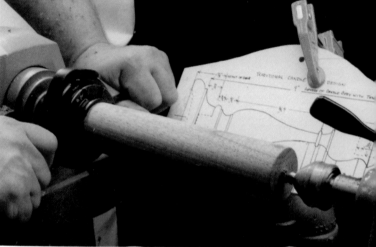

I have prepared the cylinder of wood to go into the chuck to drill the hole for the candle insert. It is much easier to perform this operation now, while we have a more substantial bulk of timber to hold. Tighten up the chuck and reinsert the live centre to check that it is running true.

Use the parting tool to square off the end.

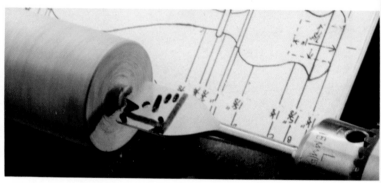

Fit a 1" drill in the tail stock's drill chuck. Drill the hole for the candle holder in 1" deep. Consideration should be given when drilling this hole to the diameter of the brass liner (if you are using one) or the size of the candles that you normally use. Note: if using sawtooth bits, slow the lathe down to avoid overheating the teeth.

Drill the hole.

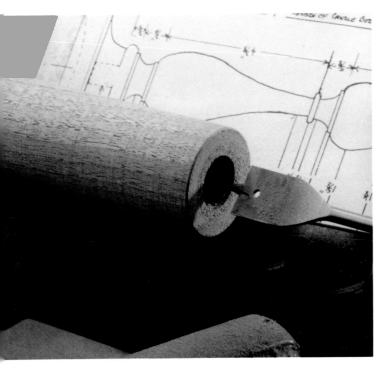

The finished hole measures one inch deep.

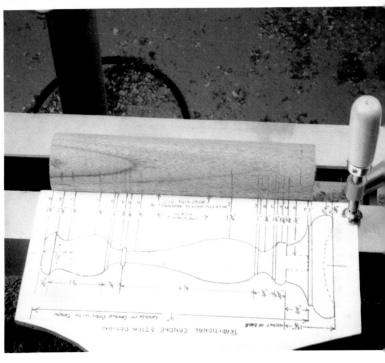

Removing the candlestick from the lathe and, using a pencil, mark in the positions of all the details from the template.

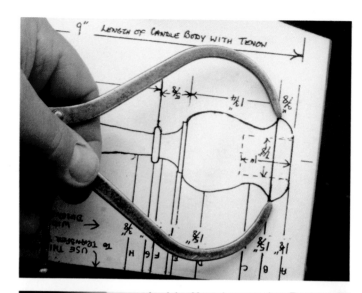

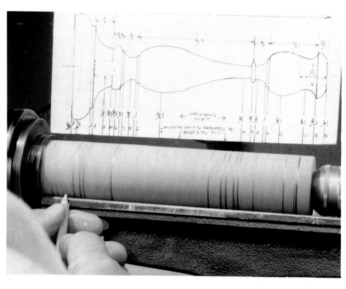

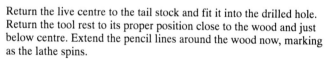

Return the live centre to the tail stock and fit it into the drilled hole. Return the tool rest to its proper position close to the wood and just below centre. Extend the pencil lines around the wood now, marking as the lathe spins.

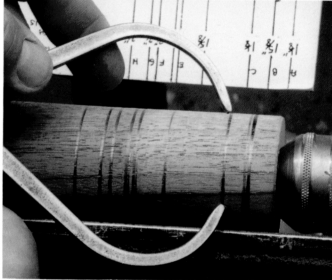

Dimension I should be the size you arrive at after you rough your 2 x 2 down into a cylinder. This will be the thickest size of the candlestick stem. Positions B and D are both 1 5/8". Use the calipers to measure as you cut down to these two high points with the parting tool.

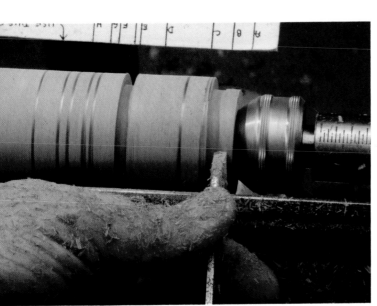

Bring the end wood down to the 1 5/8" deep cut.

Round the end.

Bring down the wood between the two cuts down to 1 5/8".

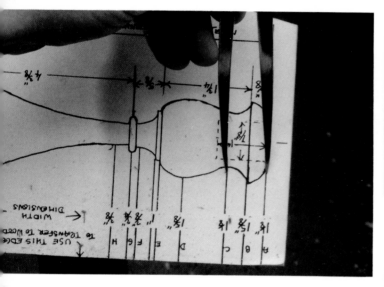

Set the dividers and remark dimension C.

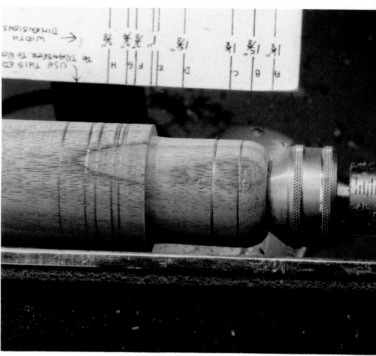

Dimensions C and B are marked in.

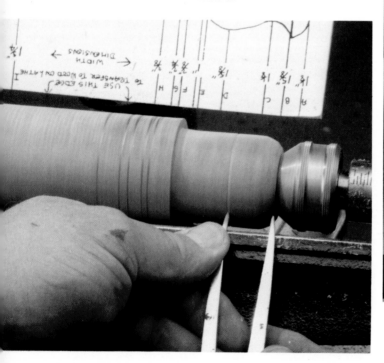

Mark this dimension on the wood. Repeat this process with dimension B.

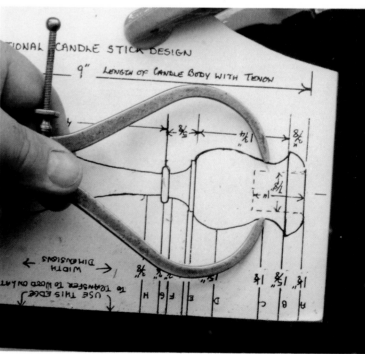

Set the caliper to the hollow at position C, measuring 1 1/8" in diameter.

The wood is reduced to 1 1/8" at position C.

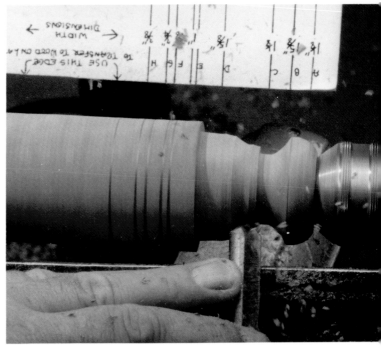

We have set dimension C, the base of the curve on the candle cup. Now we are going to turn the short curve between B & C using a small round nosed scraper. We will cut the longer curve from D to C using a gouge. Remember scrapers cut downward and gouges cut in the upward position.

35

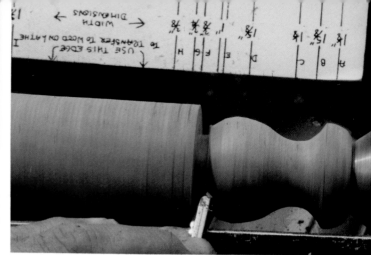

Clean this shape up using a scraper.

Roll over the curve to item E with the spindle gouge.

Move to the flange at item E. Measure it with the calipers and reduce the wood stock with your parting tool to the 1" diameter of this item, checking with the calipers as you go.

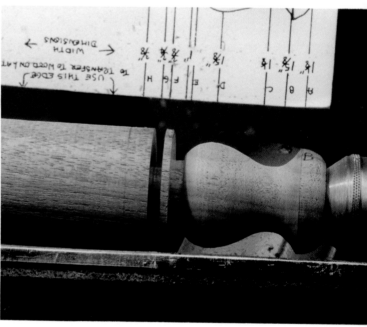

Measure in the narrow bead at item G with the calipers. Reduce the excess stock to the appropriate size with the parting tool.

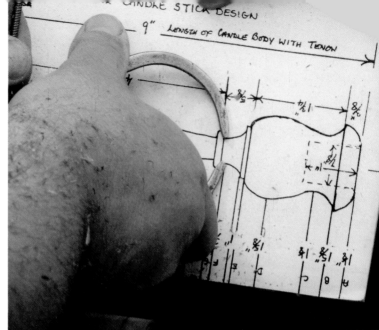

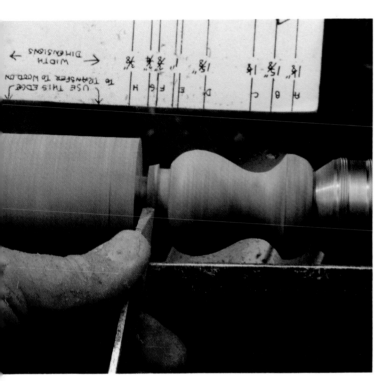

Reduce the waste wood between F & G.

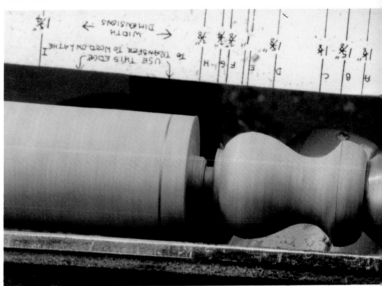

Reduce the wood on either side of the bead to 3/4" in diameter using a small parting tool and the calipers as before.

Round down the bead.

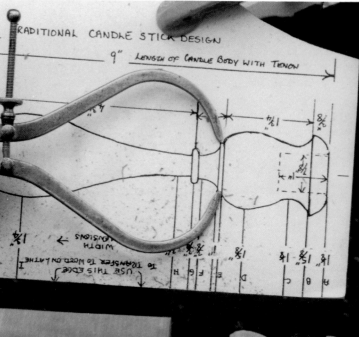

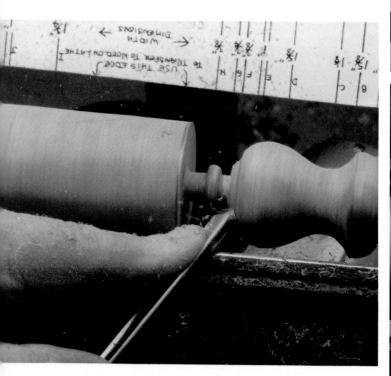

Reduce the curve between D & F with the parting tool.

Add the collar at item E.

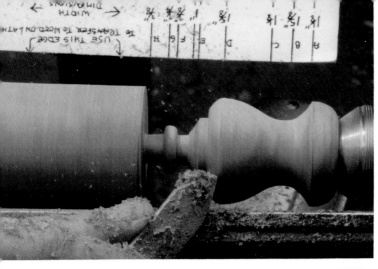

Using the parting tool, cut in bead J.

Round the shoulder above E.

Smooth the curve between E and F with the parting tool.

Cut in bead L as well.

Remove the waste wood from between these two beads with the parting tool.

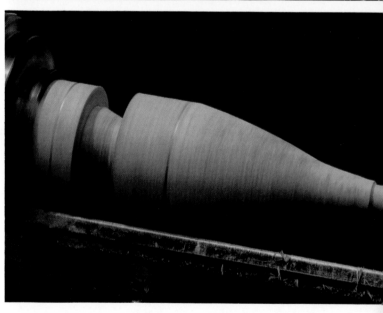

Sweep down with the rounded part of the roughing gouge from item I to H. Remember to always cut down hill to keep the compressed fibers together.

This slightly hollow taper is now in place.

Deliniate beads J and L with the parting tool.

Roll over the final edge below item I with the parting tool.

Using a small round nosed scraper, form the cove listed as item K.

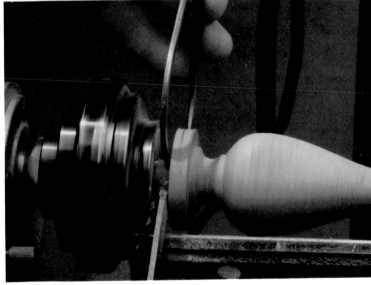

Create the tenon (1/2" in diameter) with the parting tool, measuring with the calipers.

41

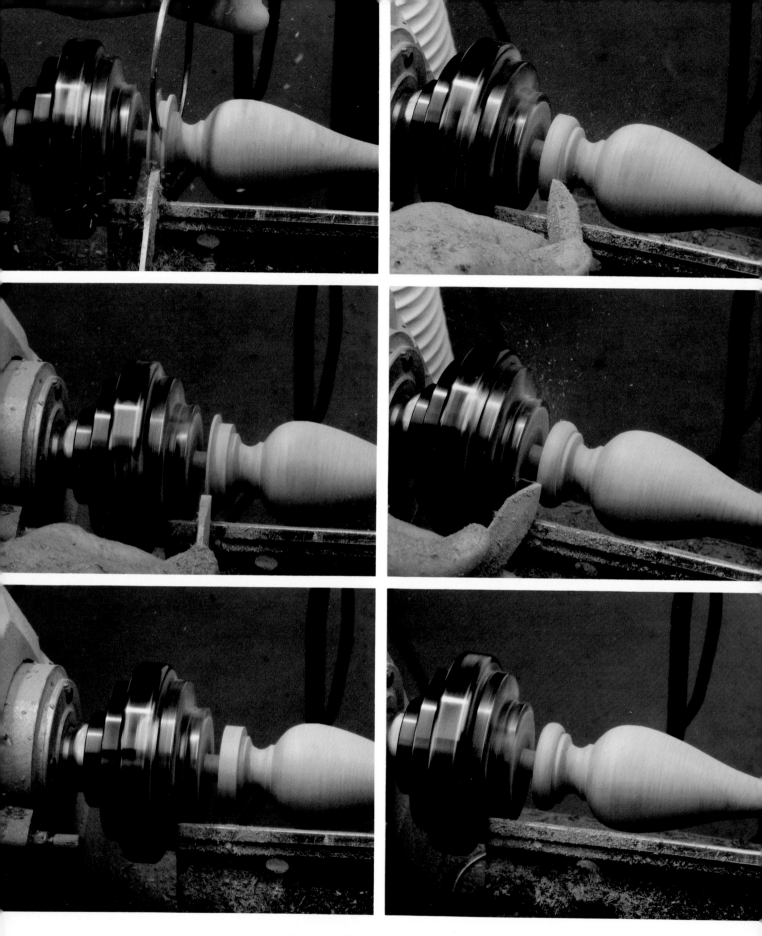

Create the final bead. First reduce the centre to the proper dimension.
Reduce the excess wood at either end. Round the top end of the bead
and then the bottom end.

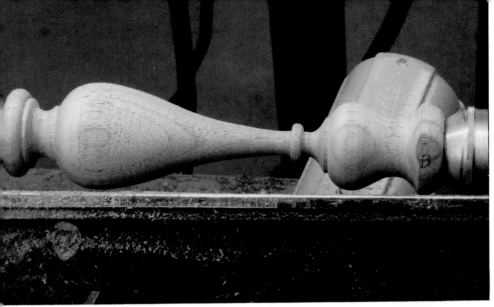

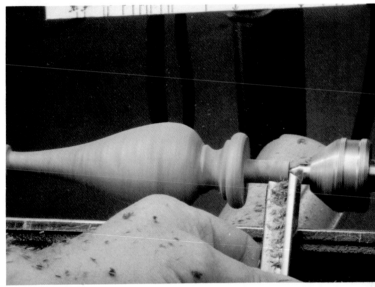

The candlestick is now almost ready to be joined with its base. Reverse the direction of the candlestick and prepare to remove the excess wood from the base (the wood which was held by the chuck).

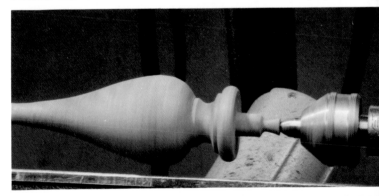

Don't forget to leave the bottom tenon in place as you reduce the excess stock.

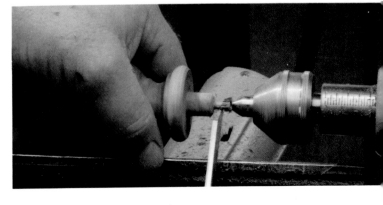

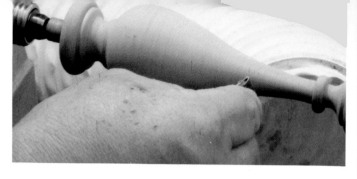

Smooth the candlestick with your abrasive papers, using the dust extractor as you go. Be careful not to blunt the sharp edges you have created where they are necessary to the design.

Using Superglue, attach the column to the base.

Using the 1/8" gouge, remove the recess to the base underneath the candlestick.

Apply Danish Oil or sealer to the candlestick.

Apply a coat of wax to give the wood a glossy appearance. Use a paper towel to apply the wax.

The finished traditional candlestick.

PREPARING THE BLANKS FOR TRIPLE CANDLESTICKS

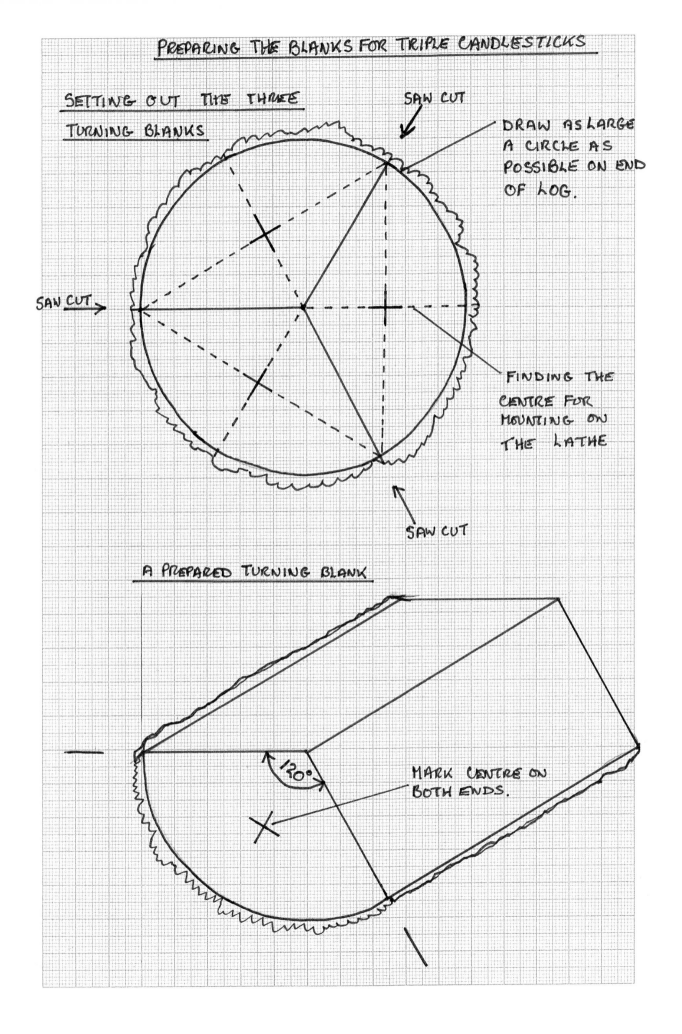

SETTING OUT THE THREE TURNING BLANKS

SAW CUT

DRAW AS LARGE A CIRCLE AS POSSIBLE ON END OF LOG.

SAW CUT

FINDING THE CENTRE FOR MOUNTING ON THE LATHE

SAW CUT

A PREPARED TURNING BLANK

120°

MARK CENTRE ON BOTH ENDS.

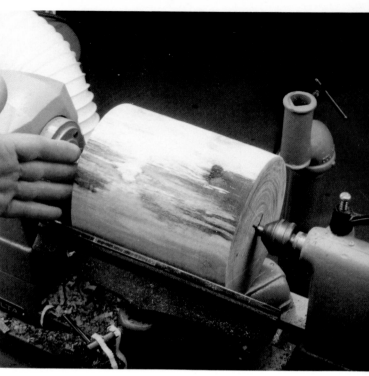

Now we are going to make three candles together from a single mimosa log measuring 7 1/2" in diameter and 8" high. This is an artistic approach to woodturning and the dimensions are not critical. This is a free-hand approach not needing careful plan drawings. Find the centre at each end of the log and place a mark at the centres with an awl. This wood is unseasoned. It is rare to find a log in the round that is seasoned.

This nicely turned log has attractive spalting patterns (created by fungus attacking the log as it lay in the wet grass).

Mount the log to the lathe with a four prong drive (you may also use a face plate ring). For this triple candlestick, I have chosen to cut the bark away and make a true cylinder first. There are other examples with the bark left on that have a different look. True up the log with the heaviest roughing gouge you have. I am using a 1" but a 3/4" would work. If this is your first attempt you may prefer to start with a smaller log, say four or five inches in diameter.

True up both ends of the log with your bowl gouge as well. The beveled edge closes and compresses the wood grain.

Move around the log from mark to mark until you have gone around the entire edge and placed six marks around the edge.

Now measure the radius of the log with dividers. Bring the divider end from the centre to the outer edge and mark that position.

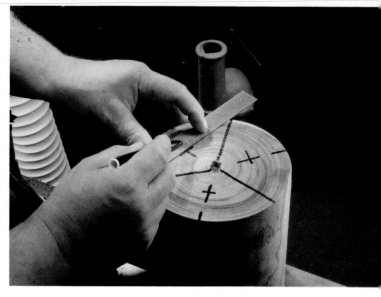

Add centres to all three of the resulting sections by first drawing a straight line between the centre and the short marks and then by placing the ruler at the tips of two of the long lines you will be able to mark the approximate centre position.

Using a bandsaw, cut the log into three sections, following the long guide lines. Have a wedge handy when making the first cut as sometimes the log closes up and grips the bandsaw blade.

Using a ruler mark these off with alternating long and short lines.

48

Place a centre mark in each centre on all three pieces of the mimosa log.

Mount one of the three mimosa sections on the lathe. Make sure the lathe speed is turned down a bit until you have this piece trued up.

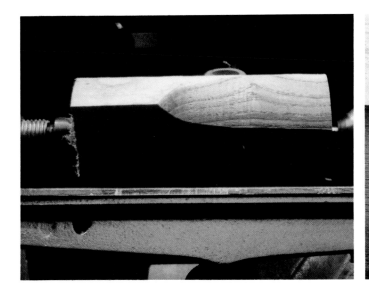

Begin rounding the wood with a large roughing gouge.

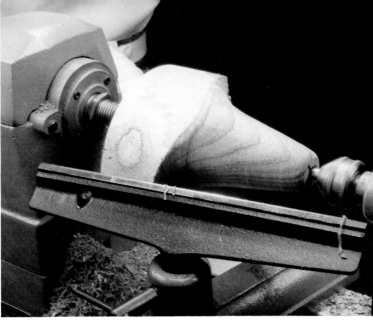

As we go we're thinning down the stem with the tool rest angled. This will give us the beginnings of a nice candlestick shape. At this stage, if your wood was really wet you would seal it with end grain sealer and store it until it had dried for several months. This log is not that wet and we will continue onward.

Cut a slot at the base of the design with the parting tool. Remember to widen your slot so the tool will not bind.

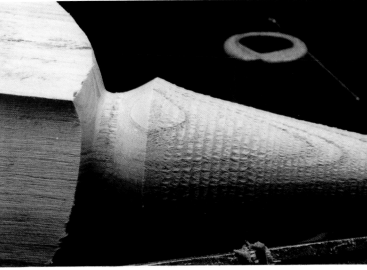

Use the 3/8" bowl gouge to create this curve above the part line.

Round over the shoulder with the scraper.

Use a scraper in a downward motion to create this curve.

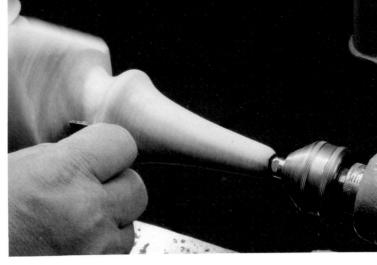

Begin to sand the stem of the candle just a little.

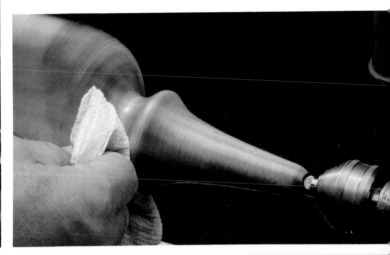

Change over to a smaller tool rest now to get in closer to the work. Use a bowl gouge to add a more graceful curve to the stem.

Round over the top end and this first candle is ready for sanding. Note that the candle base has been left in a triangular form so that all three pieces will fit together in the end.

Apply Danish Oil to the stem with a brush and buff with a paper towel.

Let's try a different design on the second candlestick of the three. Repeat the reducing steps above. Mark the shoulder from the nearly finished first candlestick so the second candlestick's shoulder will line up with the first.

Taper the candlestick down to the marks at the shoulders. Make sure the top ends of the candlesticks are approximately the same size as well.

Roll the skew chisel over from perpendicular to vertical to create this rounded end. These candlesticks are intended to have a rustic look and not to be flimsy or petite.

Form a concave curve to come in neatly to the underside of the balaster leg. I used the 3/8" bowl gouge to accomplish this, sweeping from the outside in.

Refine the shape of the piece with the skew chisel. Always follow the horizon.

Rough out the shape of the third candlestick as before. I have decided to keep this third stick very simple with an elegant sweep from the bottom to the top. Using the small tool rest and the 3/8" bowl gouge, create this gentle sweep. Begin by reducing the shoulder to the height of the other two candlesticks.

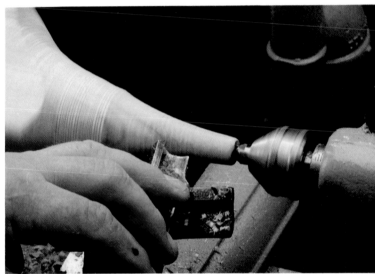

Add a curve to the stem.

Reduce the top to the the same size as the other two candlesticks.

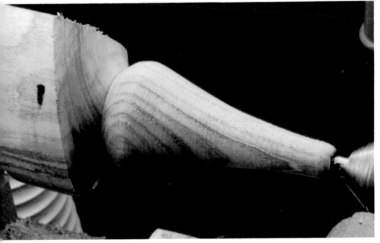

The second candlestick is ready for sanding and oil. (Three coats of oil will be required with several hours drying time in between.)

Round the end.

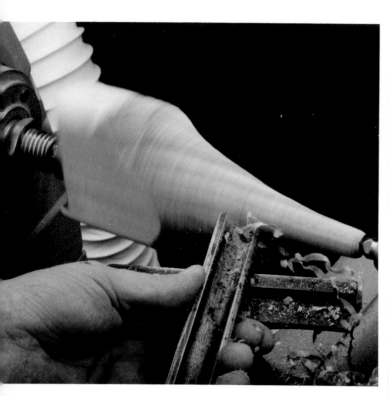

Now with the two ends determined, add a gentle sweep to the middle.

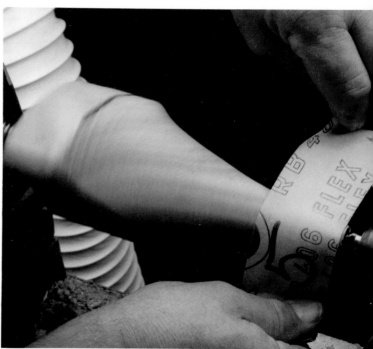

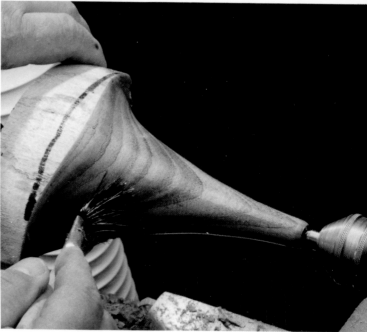

Sand and oil the third candlestick.

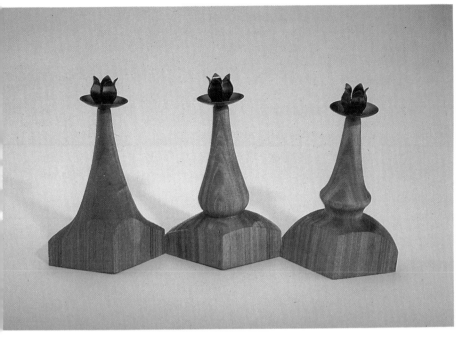

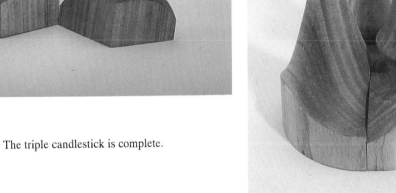

The triple candlestick is complete.

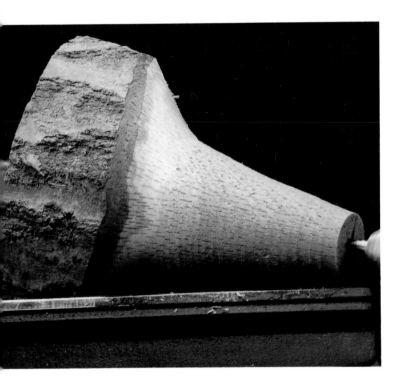

Here I am using a piece of red oak to make a similar candlestick but I will be leaving the bark on the base. This is a rough turned blank which now can be allowed to dry. This way only the amount of wood required has to dry. As the wood has been divided from the main log, all the stress factors have been removed [shrinkage] so several months later you will be able to turn up some finished candlesticks instead of waiting years. At this stage all end grain should be coated with end seal to prevent it from drying too quickly and cracking. Any splits and shakes that do develop may be glued with cyanoacrylate glue.

Gallery

A traditional candlestick turned in mopane.

A triple candlestick turned from yew wood.

The outer bark has been left in place to give this triple candlestick a different look and feel.

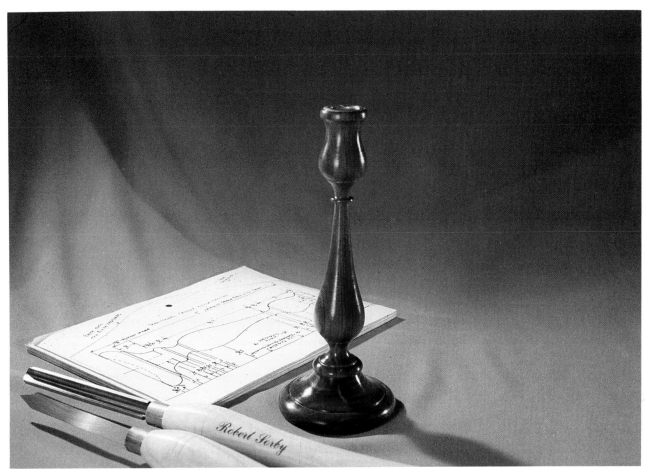

Candlesticks by Geoff Hughes.